The Worldview Series

In their Eyes

ALI NAJI

THE MAINSTAY FOUNDATION

By: The Mainstay Foundation

Printed in the United States.

ISBN: 978-1943393398

In the name of *what is true,* including *what is right,* I offer the following attempt to the last *guardian.* As we bid farewell to the month of Ramaḍān, it is bitter-sweet. But it is the occultation of your moon that pains us most. Praise the Lord of that blessed House under which the Earth was spread.

CONTENTS

Contents 1

In Their Eyes 3

Acknowledgements *5*

Now, Look Back *7*

The 12th Guardian: Living Incognito *13*

The 11th Guardian: Preparing for the Awaited One *16*

The 10th Guardian: Guiding Despite Persecution *21*

The 9th Guardian: Leading from his Earliest Years *25*

The 8th Guardian: Being the Most Content *29*

The 7th Guardian: Holding Back without Holding Back *35*

The 6th Guardian: Teaching on a Wider-scale *41*

The 5th Guardian: Planting the Seeds *49*

The 4th Guardian: Reminding Through Worship *55*

The 3rd Guardian: Subsisting After Existing *61*

The 2nd Guardian: Enjoying the Love of the Most Beloved *67*

The 1st Guardian: Guarding the Qurʾān *71*

IN THEIR EYES

Acknowledgements

Being self-aware regarding the influence of multiple factors on my use of language, terms, categories and frameworks is in order.[1] Although truth is out there for any sincere seeker, we seldom journey in a vacuum. For the ensuing reflections, I am thus indebted to various gracious souls, communities, and environments. First and foremost, I thank the truth for being there in a way that is accessible to some extent, regardless of all else. I thank my loving parents, supportive family and reliable friends, especially my beloved wife. I am forever grateful to my mentors and educators. Institutions and communities of learning across time and space command my lasting gratitude and reverence. I extend special appreciation to the Mainstay Foundation and its editorial team for supporting this project. To those I have neglected proper recognition and thanks, I cannot truly do you justice. As the wise have said, "How can I truly thank you when being able to say, 'thank you,' calls for another, 'thank you'?"[2] Any good in my work is yours and the shortcomings are all my own.

Now, Look Back

Your living miracle has brought you this far. You are unstoppable now – so long as you nurture this insight. The present moment expands forward and backward in time. You are in a journey towards infinite, there is no turning back. But with the clarity of this moment, you can now peek into the past. You have a living miracle, you have a living *guardian* – even if only behind the scenes – and you have a *guarded* community.[3] This awareness is a critical vision, a discerning mechanism, granting you access to the past in ways that others simply lack. If many supposedly "historical" records were influenced by tyrants, how do we tell what is true from false? Put aside petty details; I'm speaking of the core events. What about those turning points in history that govern our spiritual program today? What about the transition from *chosen one* to succeeding *guardian* and from *guardian* to subsequent *guardian*? What about that framework of human guidance, delivered and protected? When different versions of events are accounted by rivaling groups, how does a seeker of truth find the surest way home? We are like detectives searching for clues, for traces, for evidence... But the difference between us and other detectives is that we feel the presence of a living miracle as well as a living *guardian*. This aids us in determining the correct version of events crucial for guidance. Indeed, a version of events that *does not make sense* cannot be true.

For example, wisdom dictates that a living *guardian* – executing God's will day-to-day, at least behind the scenes – *must* exist after the final *chosen one.* This Imam, this vicegerent, is a pure conduit for the enactment of God's will on a constant basis.[4] So, any version of events that contradicts this must be false. On the flipside, a narrative that coincides with said truth is more likely to be veracious. If there is only one surviving narrative that matches up with the aforementioned principle, then – by process of elimination – it is the truth. For the core game-changing truths must be guarded infallibly in order to maintain humanity's fair chance at guidance. The living *guardian* of the message is an intuitively game-changing fact. With him, there is someone who lives up to the message to the fullest and who guards it behind the scenes. Without him, there is no one ready to lead with *all* the correct answers when people are ready to submit to the truth. Without him, there is no physical guarantor that the critical threshold of guidance is intact. The active *guardian* may choose to administer affairs according to overriding priorities, keeping some things confidential or characterized by limited-access, but only by recognizing the indispensable role of that living *guardian* can all these other pieces of the puzzle fall into place. *The living guardian can accommodate and manage threats to the details.*[5] *But without this living, physical link, known as the Immaculate Imam, the one living up to the message to the fullest would be non-existent and the bar of accessible guidance would be – incorrectly – too low.* Knowing the necessity of the impeccable *guardian*'s presence helps us to see what other detectives may not always be able to see when it comes to piecing together accounts of history.

With this present awareness, let us look back. The warmth of the sun, despite being concealed by the clouds, reveals a truth beyond skepticism – the light shines on because its source has never stopped powering it up. Light upon light, the shining light of this moment tells an ancient story – if only I listen with cognition. Let us look back to the 12 Imams of the *guarded* community, with the final Imam at the forefront, albeit behind the scenes, as he is today. Let us look back... But let us look back to see snapshots of how even some of those outside the *guarded* community saw these 12 Imams... With the insight energized thus far, such testimonies can intensify the certainty that this series of 12 *guardians* is like none other... Unmatched, unsurpassed. Follow the references for more information.

Every age has its *guardian.* The innocent hearts and minds of humankind can sense this and realize its ramifications. Almost 1400 years ago, the last *chosen one* confirmed it and prophesied the reign of 12 *guardians,* one after the other.[6] Their mention is not absent from the scriptures of old.[7] They lead in the realm of guidance and spirituality even when oppressors keep them from taking their rightful place as temporal rulers.

The 12th Imam[8] is the *guardian* prophesied to usher in world peace. Long have the oppressed anticipated his birth and, till this day, they await the fruition of his mission. Like Jesus[9] in his guidance at a young age, like Noah[10] in his long life and venerable wisdom, like Joseph[11] in his hidden identity, the 12th Imam leads an extended life of secrecy. It has been many centuries since the 12th and last *guardian* was born. Despite the tight security situation, enough close confidants of the 11th Imam had learned of the awaited one's birth and spread the news throughout the *guarded community* when the time was right.

The 12th *Guardian*: Living Incognito

But even beyond the *guarded community*, many recognized this special birth. Although these outsider testimonies did not necessarily recognize the 12th Imam as an impeccable *guardian* per se, some identified him as a distinguished leader or the prophesied *Mahdī* (the rightly guided one). The Mahdī, as a savior figure, would spread fairness and justice across the globe, according to the last *chosen one*.[12] For example[13], there are indications that Aḥmad ibn Muḥammad al-Balādhurī (d. 339

AH)[14] not only referred to the 12th Imam by name as "Muḥammad son of Ḥasan[15] son of ʿAlī[16]", but in doing so also claimed to have transmitted a report from the 12th Imam, calling him, "the leader[17] of his age."[18]

We live in the age of the 12th *guardian*. It has been many centuries now that the 12th *guardian* has upheld his roles in a covert fashion. Initially, he would communicate with the *guarded community* through specifically designated ambassadors. This relatively short period (260 AH – 329 AH)[19] proved to be a significant transition into the extended period[20] of the 12th Imam's life incognito. During the latter era, the 12th Imam watches over the *guarded community* only behind the scenes, in disguise or by proxy, with no public point of communication. For practical questions during this extended period, the *guarded community* of Twelver Shīʿīs is left to the reasonable practice of referring to qualified specialists. According to some reports, the 12th Imam wrote,

[...] أما الحوادث الواقعة فارجعوا فيها إلى رواة حديثنا

فإنهم حجتي عليكم وأنا حجة الله عليهم .[...]

[...] As for the [occurrences/events/incidents][21] that occur, refer[22] – concerning them – to the [scholarly][23] transmitters[24] of our [words/traditions][25], for they are my [proof of my favor][26] upon you and I am the [proof of the favor][27] of God upon them. [...][28]

The 11th *Guardian*: Preparing for the Awaited One

As the reader will soon realize, these were by no means abrupt transitions. The famous historian al-Masʿūdī (d. ca 345 AH) writes in his *Ithbāt al-Waṣiyyah*,

وروي أنّ أبا الحسن صاحب العسكر [عليه السلام] احتجب عن كثير من الشيعة إلّا عن عدد يسير من خواصّه، فلمّا افضي الأمر إلى أبي محمّد عليه السلام كان يكلّم شيعته الخواصّ وغيرهم من وراء الستر إلّا في الأوقات الّتي يركب فيها إلى دار السلطان، وإنّ ذلك إنّما كان منه ومن أبيه قبله مقدّمة لغيبة صاحب الزمان، لتألف الشيعة ذلك ولا تنكر الغيبة، وتجري العادة بالاحتجاب والاستتار

> *It has been reported that [the 10th Imam][29] kept himself hidden from [much[30] of the guarded community[31]] except for a small number of his confidants. Then when [the guardianship][32] went to [his son, the 11th Imam][33], he would communicate with [even] his confidants [of the guarded community[34]] as well as others [only] behind the veil [of secrecy] except for the times in which he would ride to the [sultan's place]. He and his father before him would do so as a primer for the [12th Imam's period of secrecy][35] such that the [guarded community] may become accustomed to it and not deny [the period of secrecy]; and so that the secrecy and concealment becomes a norm.*[36]

The roles of the 10th and 11th Imams were pivotal in paving the way for the 12th Imam's underground mission.

Despite the short duration[37] of his active *guardianship,* even outside the *guarded community* many praised the standing of the 11th *guardian*. For example, al-Jāḥiẓ (d. 255 AH) mentions the 11th Imam among a unique lineage of ten erudite sages[38], each with prominent, "scholarship, asceticism, worship, courage, generosity, purity, and spiritual prosperity." This author is not a Twelver Shīʿī but holds these individuals in high regard, naming them one after the other, starting with the 11th *guardian*,

وهم: الحسن بن علي بن محمد بن علي بن موسى بن جعفر بن محمد بن علي بن الحسين بن علي. وهذا لم يتفق لبيت من بيوت العرب ولا من بيوت العجم

> *And they are: Ḥasan[39], son of ʿAlī[40], son of Muḥammad[41], son of ʿAlī[42], son of Mūsá[43], son of Jaʿfar[44], son of Muḥammad[45], son of ʿAlī[46], son of Ḥusayn[47], son of ʿAlī[48]. This has not been the case for any [other] household, neither among the Arabs nor among the [non-Arabs][49].*[50]

Al-Jāḥiẓ is pointing out the exceptionality of having so many praiseworthy personalities hail from a single hereditary line consecutively. Moreover, in his *Tadhkirat al-Khawāṣ,* Sibṭ ibn al-Jawzī (d. 654 AH) – another scholar *not* from the *guarded community* – describes the 11th *guardian* as, "a trustworthy, erudite sage[51], who transmitted sayings/traditions from his father and grandfather [...]."[52]

The 10th *Guardian*: Guiding Despite Persecution

The 10th Imam[53] along with the 11th Imam are often referred to as *al-ʿAskarīyān* (sing. *Al-ʿAskarī*), meaning, "the two associated with *al-ʿAskar*." *Al-ʿAskar* is a term related to the armed forces and, in this context, is commonly understood in reference to Samarra, Iraq, where the ʿAbbāsid ruler stationed his troops and kept a close watch on these two Imams.[54] The non-Shīʿī author, Yāqūt al-Ḥamawī (d. 626 AH), attests to the reason these two Imams were called *al-ʿAskarīyān*, while also referring to, "their descendant, the awaited one[55] [...]".[56] Regarding the 10th Imam, al-Dhahabī (d. 748 AH) – another scholar from outside the *guarded community* – writes,

[254 هـ:] وفيها أبو الحسن علي بن الجواد محمد بن الرضى علي بن الكاظم موسى بن الصادق جعفر العلوي الحسيني المعروف بالهادي، توفي بسامرا وله أربعون سنة. وكان فقيهاً إماماً متعبداً [...]

[254 AH:] In this [year], Abū al-Ḥasan[57] ʿAlī[58] – son of the generous one[59] Muḥammad[60], son of the content one[61] ʿAlī[62], son of the forbearing one[63] Mūsá[64], son of the honest one[65] Jaʿfar[66] – the [descendant of Ḥusayn[67], the descendent of ʿAlī[68]], the one[69] known as the guide[70], passed away in Samarra at the age of 40.[71] He was an erudite scholar[72], a leader[73], and one of dedicated worship[74].[...][75]

Given the attributes listed in this quotation, al-Dhahabī recognizes the 10th Imam as a notable leader, in knowledge and piety. Nonetheless, he rejects the notion that he or any of the remaining 11 Imams are infallible guardians. This author and others like him outside the *guarded community* did not recognize the need for a *guardian* of every age, identified as one of the 12 Imams, a member of the last *chosen one*'s Household[76] who would guard and represent the Qurʾān impeccably. May *the one with no need* help us always open our hearts and minds to the truth.

The 9th *Guardian*: Leading from his Earliest Years

At such a young age, the 12th *guardian* was vested with the task of upholding the message of Islam. His grandfather before him, that is the 10th *guardian,* had faced a similar responsibility at less than ten years of age. It is the 9th *guardian*[77], however, who had the earlier precedent of active *guardianship* in his youth. Believers from the *guarded community* came to terms with this leadership partly because the miraculous Qur'ān gave an example making it clear that age was not a hindrance in the face of God's will. God inspired the *chosen one,* Jesus son of Mary, to speak despite being only a baby in the cradle.[78] If Divine Wisdom dictates it, just as a *chosen one* – of any age – can act as a conduit for God's message, so can a *guardian* – of any age – intervene to protect God's message.

In his *Tāriīkh al-Islām*, al-Dhahabī (d. 748 AH) writes the following about the 9th Imam,

[...] كان من سروات آل بيت النبي [...]. وكان أحد الموصوفين بالسخاء ، ولذلك لقب بالجواد. [...]

> *[...] He was among the honorable figures of the Prophet's Household [...]. He was one of those known for his generosity, and that is why he was given the title al-Jawād (the generous one). [...]*[79]

This was a reputation the 9th *guardian* had accumulated before he departed this world at the tender age of 25. Muḥammad ibn Ṭalḥah al-Shāfiʿī (d. 652 AH), also from outside the *guarded community*, tells us that,

وإن كان صغير السن فهو كبير القدر رفيع الذكر.

Despite his young age, he is of great standing [and] high eminence.[80]

Ibn al-Ṣabbāgh al-Mālikī (d. 855 AH) quotes this excerpt from *Maṭālib al-Sa ʾūl* in his own work, *al-Fuṣūl al-Muhimmah Fī Ma ʿrifat al-A ʾimmah.*[81] Because the *guardian* shines by the will of *the one with no need,* no matter how much the wrongdoers attempt to put out that light, its warmth is still felt.[82] Describing the 9th Imam, Sibṭ ibn al-Jawzī (d. 654 AH) writes,

وكان على منهاج أبيه في العلم والتقى والزهد والجود

[...]

And he followed his father's footsteps in his knowledge, piety, asceticism, and generosity [...][83]

What was so exceptional about the 8th Imam such that he became the reference point for describing the 9th Imam?

The 8th *Guardian*: Being the Most Content

As Sibṭ ibn al-Jawzī (d. 654 AH) relays, the historian al-Wāqidī (d. 207 AH) describes the 8th Imam[84] as a trusted scholar even in his early twenties,

سمع علي الحديث من أبيه وعمومته وغيرهم وكان ثقة يفتي بمسجد رسول الله [ص] وهو ابن نيف وعشرين سنة [...]

ʿAlī[85] heard [words/traditions][86] from his father[87], uncles, and others; he was trustworthy and used to [scholarly] answer questions [on matters of religion][88] in the mosque of God's Messenger[89] [pbuh][90] at [only] a little over twenty years of age [...][91]

The "hearing" involved here is not merely an auditory experience. It is shorthand for the process of passing down the previous generation's knowledge of the prophetic tradition. Ibn Abī al-Ḥadīd al-Muʿtazilī (d. 656 AH) speaks of our 8th *guardian* as a man of unmatched merit,

[...] كان أعلم الناس وأسخى الناس وأكرم الناس أخلاقًا.

[...] He was the most learned of the people; the most generous of the people; and the most honorable of the people in [his character/moral conduct][92].[93]

This testimony should suffice as a decisive argument in favor of the 8th Imam's leadership. For if those outside the *guarded community* do not recognize the need for an *impeccable guardian*, at the very least they must admit the necessity of deferring to the authority of the *most qualified* leader.[94] Too much is at stake to settle for anyone less than the best. Whose credentials surpass those of one with superior knowledge and character?

Ibn Ḥibbān (d. 354 AH), yet another scholar *not* associated with the *guarded community*, writes the following about the 8th Imam in his *al-Thuqāt*,

> [...] من سادات أهل البيت وعقلائهم وجلة الهاشميين ونبلائهم [...] ومات علي بن موسى الرضا بطوس من شربة سقاه إياها المأمون فمات من ساعته [...] وقبره بسناباذ خارج النوقان مشهور يزار بجنب قبر الرشيد قد زرته مرارا كثيرة وما حلت بي شدة في وقت مقامي بطوس فزرت قبر علي بن موسى الرضا صلوات الله على جده وعليه ودعوت الله إزالتها عنى إلا أستجيب لي وزالت عنى تلك الشدة وهذا شئ جربته مرارا

فوجدته كذلك أماتنا الله على محبة المصطفى وأهل بيته صلى الله عليه وسلم الله عليه وعليهم أجمعين.

[...] He was among the [leading and intellectual figures] of the [Prophet's] Household[95]*, [among] the majestic and noble personalities of the Hāshimīs*[96] *[...] ʿAlī son of Mūsá, the content one*[97]*, died in Ṭūs*[98] *due to a [poisoned] drink given to him by [the ʿAbbāsid ruler] al-Maʾmūn*[99]*, [leading to his death at the time]. [...] His grave is in Sanābādh, outside al-Nūqān*[100]*; a famous destination that is visited; next to the grave of [the ʿAbbāsid ruler Hārūn] al-Rashīd*[101]*. I have visited [his grave] again and again, many times. If ever a difficulty has befallen me during my stay in Ṭūs, when I would visit the grave of ʿAlī son of Mūsá, the content one*[102]*, may God's blessings shower upon his grandfather and upon him, and I would pray to God to relieve me of it, then my prayers would always be answered and I would be relieved*

of that difficulty. This is something I have tried time and time again, and I have found it to be so. May God have us depart this life in a state of love for [the last] chosen one[103] *and his Household*[104]*, may God's peace and blessings shower upon him and upon them all.*[105]

Ibn Ḥibbān is willing to vouch for the 8th *guardian* to this extent, but warns us not to accept the "false" reports ascribed to him as transmitted by, "his descendants and followers."[106] Did all his descendants and followers plot to tell a lie when they claimed to relay the words and actions of their Imam? The reputation of the subsequent Imams (those we have discussed thus far), alone, debunks this claim. Furthermore, the bigger picture[107] only makes sense if we recognize this Imam's special status as a trace of his *guardianship*, being one of the 12 prophesied *guardians*, anticipated caretakers of the holy Qurʾān, and Divinely appointed Imams prepared to lead impeccably when people are ready for the next step.

The 7th *Guardian*: Holding Back without Holding Back

Ibn Abī Ḥātim al-Rāzī (d. 327 AH) reports that his father Abū Ḥātim (d. 277 AH) – both authorities outside the *guarded community* – describes the 7th Imam[108] as follows,

ثقة صدوق امام من أئمة المسلمين

A trustworthy, honest one; a leader[109] among the Muslim leaders[110]

Fakhr al-Dīn al-Rāzī (d. 604 AH), another leading authority for many Muslims outside the *guarded community*, describes the 8th Imam and three of his forefathers as men of immense erudition. As he puts it in his *Tafsīr*,

[...] ثم انظر كم كان فيهم من الأكابر من العلماء كالباقر والصادق والكاظم والرضا [...]

> *[...] then look at how many giant erudite scholars there were among them, such as the revealer [of knowledge][111], the honest one[112], the forbearing one[113], the content one[114], peace be upon them [...][115]*

Al-Kāẓim, the forbearing one, the one who holds back his anger, was the 7th *guardian*. The historian al-Khaṭīb al-Baghdādī (d. 463 AH) reports,

كان موسى بن جعفر يدعي العبد الصالح من عبادته واجتهاده. روى أصحابنا أنه دخل مسجد رسول الله صلى الله عليه وسلم فسجد سجدة في أول الليل، وسمع وهو يقول في سجوده: عظيم الذنب عندي فليحسن

العفو عندك. يا أهل التقوى ويا أهل المغفرة. فجعل يرددها حتى أصبح، وكان سخيا كريما [...]

Mūsá son of Jaʿfar[116] *was called "the righteous servant"*[117] *for his [devoted] worship and dedicated effort [to that end]. Our fellows have reported that [when] he entered the mosque of God's Messenger, he prostrated*[118] *at the beginning of the night and, while in a state of prostration, he was heard saying, "Immense is the fault [on my end], so let the pardon be beautiful [on Your end]. O You who are worthy of [us] being mindful*[119] *[of You], and O You who it is befitting of You to forgive [us]." He would repeat that until the morning. And he was charitable, generous [...]*[120]

The image presented of the 7th Imam is one of a distinctly pious sage. The prayer recounted here emphasizes the spirit of reverence this individual had before God's humbling presence. Feeling God's unlimited favor entails a profound sense of shortcoming on the part of a limited being, making him feel at "fault" despite being impeccably devout. Actually, this experience can be seen as the sign of his eminent spirituality. Muḥammad ibn Ṭalḥah al-Shāfiʿī (d. 652 AH) writes,

[...] ولفرط حلمه وتجاوزه عن المعتدين عليه دعي كاظما، كان يجازى المسيء بإحسانه إليه ويقابل الجاني بعفوه عنه [...] ويعرف بالعراق باب الحوائج إلى الله لنجح مطالب المتوسلين إلى الله تعالى به، كرامته تحار منها العقول، وتقضي بأن له عند الله تعالى قدم صدق لا تزل ولا تزول. [...]

[...] due to the extent of his forbearance and pardoning of those wronging him, he was called the forbearing one[121]*. He used to deal with the one who wronged him by being kind to him and he would confront the criminal with pardoning him [...] He is known in Iraq as "the gateway of needs to be fulfilled by God" because the requests of those beseeching God Almighty through*

him would be fulfilled. His honor[122] *is mindboggling and entails that he has a true [station of closeness] to God, one that does not falter or change. [...]*[123]

The 6th Guardian: Teaching on a Wider-scale

Abū Ḥanīfah al-Nuʿmān (d. 150 AH), a leading authority outside the *guarded community* and father of the *Ḥanafī* school of jurisprudence, is reported to have been asked about the most learned scholar he has seen. In response, Abū Ḥanīfah said,

ما رأيت أحدا أفقه من جعفر بن محمد [...]

I have not seen anyone more knowledgeable[124] than Jaʿfar[125] son of Muḥammad[126] [...][127]

This was the 6th Imam, "the honest one[128]," as he would be remembered perpetually. Abū Ḥanīfah continued to say,

[...] لما أقدمه المنصور الحيرة بعث إلي فقال يا أبا حنيفة ان الناس قد فتنوا بجعفر بن محمد فهيئ له من مسائلك تلك الصعاب فقال فهيأت له أربعين مسألة ثم بعث إلي أبو جعفر فأتيته بالحيرة فدخلت عليه وجعفر جالس عن يمينه فلما بصرت بهما دخلني لجعفر من الهيبة ما لم يدخلني لأبي جعفر فسلمت وأذن لي أبو جعفر فجلست ثم التفت إلى جعفر فقال يا أبا عبد الله تعرف هذا قال نعم هذا أبو حنيفة ثم أتبعها قد أتانا ثم قال يا أبا حنيفة هات من مسائلك سل أبا عبد الله فابتدأت أسأله قال فكان يقول في المسألة أنتم تقولون فيها كذا وكذا وأهل المدينة يقولون كذا ونحن نقول كذا فربما تابعنا وربما تابع أهل المدينة وربما خالفنا جميعا حتى أتيت على أربعين مسألة ما أخرج منها مسألة [...]

When [the ʿAbbāsid ruler] al-Manṣūr[129] *had [the 6th Imam] brought to al-Ḥīrah*[130] *he sent for me and said, "O Abā Ḥanīfah, people have been swayed*[131] *by Jaʿfar*[132] *son of Muḥammad*[133]*, so prepare some of those difficult questions of yours for him."*[134] *So I prepared forty questions for him. Then [al-Manṣūr]*[135] *sent for me. So I came to [see him] in al-Ḥīrah and when I came in, Jaʿfar*[136] *was sitting to his right. When I saw them both, I felt [the vibe of] Jaʿfar's [majestic presence]*[137] *more than what I felt regarding [al-Manṣūr's]. Then I greeted [them]. [Al-Manṣūr] gave me permission [to proceed], so I sat. Then [al-Manṣūr] turned to Jaʿfar and said, "O Abā ʿAbdillāh*[138]*, do you know this [person]?" [Jaʿfar] replied, "Yes, this is Abū Ḥanīfah." Then he*[139] *followed up, saying, "He has come to [see] us." Then [al-Manṣūr] said, "O Abā Ḥanīfah, [let's hear] some of your questions, ask Abā ʿAbdillāh." So I began to ask him. [In response to a question, Jaʿfar]* *would say, "You say so and so about it, the people of Madīnah*[140] *say so and so, and we say so and so." In some answers he might have our view, in others he might have the people of Madīnah's view, and in yet others he may differ with all of us. [I continued as such] until I covered forty questions, not omitting [even] a single question.*[141]

Abū Ḥanīfah reportedly concluded saying,

أليس قد روينا أن أعلم الناس أعلمهم باختلاف الناس

Haven't we conveyed that the most learned of people is the [one] most learned regarding the differences among people [?!][142]

A testimony from Abū Ḥanīfah has its weight outside the *guarded community* and reveals a glimpse of the 6th Imam's scholarly stature. Although the 6th *guardian* is much more than a knowledgeable scholar to the *guarded community*, outside of the *guarded community* this testimony indicates he was seen as no less than the most learned sage of his age.

Mālik ibn Anas (d. 179 AH), father of the *Mālikī* school of jurisprudence, is reported to have described the 6th Imam in saintly terms. In his book, *al-Shifā bi Taʿrīf Ḥuqūq al-Muṣtafá*, the *Mālikī* judge ʿIyāḍ (d. 544 AH) relays Mālik's words,

ولقد كنت أرى جعفر بن محمد وكان كثير الدعابة والتبسم فإذا ذكر عنده النبي صلى الله عليه وسلم اصفر وما رأيته يحدث عن رسول الله صلى الله عليه وسلم إلا على طهارة ، ولقد اختلفت إليه زمانا فما كنت أراه إلا على ثلاث خصال إما مصليا وإما صامتا وإما يقرأ القرآن ولا يتكلم فيما لا يعنيه وكان من العلماء والعباد الذين يخشون الله عز وجل

And I used to see Jaʿfar son of Muḥammad – he had much of a playful [sense of humor] and would smile a great deal. [Yet,] when the Prophet[143] [pbuh] was mentioned in his presence, [his physical appearance would change][144]. I have also never seen

> *him relay words on behalf of the Messenger of God[145] [pbuh] except in a state of ritual purity. For a time, I used to go to [see] him, and I did not see him except [identifiable] by one of three traits: either in a state of prayer; or in a state of silence[146]; or in a state of reciting the Qur'ān. He would not speak about something that was none of his concern. He was among the erudite sages[147] and devout worshippers who feared God Almighty.[148]*

When the founding fathers of jurisprudential schools outside the *guarded community* attest to the 6th Imam's erudite superiority and spiritual eminence, is any further comment necessary? This work intends, mainly, to uncover these testimonies – these artifacts, if you will – from the depths of oblivion and marginalization. Rendering them, faithfully, in the language of the reader suffices in making the point. The reader is well-capable of seeing the broader scheme of things in light of the previous booklets in this series.

It was during the days of this *guardian,* Imam Jaʿfar son of Muḥammad, that power transitioned from the Umayyad dynasty to the ʿAbbāsid dynasty. This period allowed the 6th Imam to propagate knowledge on a wide-scale. The *guarded community* is often associated with this Imam in particular and, thus, called the *Jaʿfarīyyah* or the *Jaʿfarīs*.

The 5th Guardian: Planting the Seeds

Al-Jāḥiẓ (d. 255 AH), a notable author with allegiances outside the *guarded community*, describes the 6th *guardian*'s predecessor, Muḥammad[149] son of ʿAlī[150], as "the revealer"[151] of knowledge,

[...] وهو سيد فقهاء الحجاز، ومنه ومن ابنه جعفر تعلم الناس الفقه، وهو الملقب بالباقر، باقر العلم [...]

[...] And he is the master of erudite scholars[152] in al-Ḥijāz[153]; it was from him

> *and his son Jaʿfar that people learned religious knowledge*[154]*; he is the one nicknamed "the revealer," [that is] the revealer of knowledge [...]*[155]

This quote hints at the distinct intellectual period which the 6th Imam fostered and for which the 5th Imam planted the seeds. It was an opportune time for these *guardians* to make knowledge accessible in ways that previous generations lacked. The oppression at the hands of the Umayyads and sensitivities within the fragile Muslim community had forced the earlier *guardians* to prioritize and be wisely selective about what information they would disclose publicly. Much of the references for religious knowledge during later periods of the *guarded community* are traced back to the 5th and 6th Imams, indicating that their circumstances allowed for more widespread propagation of knowledge compared to many earlier and subsequent Imams.

Al-Jāḥiẓ continues to relay a prophecy by the last *chosen one* regarding this knowledge revealer,

[...] لقبه به رسول الله صلى الله عليه وسلم ولم يخلق بعد، وبشر به ووعد جابر بن عبد الله برؤيته وقال: ستراه طفلًا فإذا رأيته فأبلغه عني السلام، فعاش جابر حتى رآه وقال له ما وصى به.

> *[...] It was the Messenger of God [pbuh] who nicknamed him that even before he was born; he gave glad tidings about him and promised [his companion] Jābir ibn ʿAbd Allāh*[156] *that he would [live to] see him. And he said, "You will [live to] see him as a child. So when you see him, deliver my [greetings of] peace to him." Jābir lived to see him and told him what the Messenger of God had wished.*[157]

This is a reference from outside the *guarded community* indicating that the last *chosen one* foretold of the 5th Imam's extraordinary knowledge. The long life of Jābir would serve as a vehicle to confirm something more than special about the 5th *guardian*.

Another authority not within the *guarded community* testifies to a snapshot of the 5th Imam's spiritual aura. In his *Ḥilyat al-Awliyāʾ wa Ṭabaqāt al-Aṣfiyāʾ*, Aḥmad ibn ʿAbd Allāh al-Aṣfahānī (d. 430 AH) writes,

ومنهم الحاضر الذاكر، الخاشع الصابر، أبو جعفر محمد بن علي الباقر، كان من سلالة النبوة، وممن جمع حسب الدين والأبوة [...]

> *And among [the friends of God] is the one of presence and remembrance, the one of humbleness and patience – [that is] Abū Jaʿfar[158], Muḥammad son of ʿAlī; he was from the lineage of the chosen ones[159] and among those who enjoyed the honor of both [stature in] faith and [nobility in] ancestry [...][160]*

Each of the attributes in this short excerpt summarizes multitudes of ethical and spiritual ideals. Sensing the presence of *the one with no need* is a key to immaculate choice-making. True mention of God manifests not only in thoughts and in words but in every action... This is a man whose impeccable choices renew the legacy of his noble lineage. He is not revered merely because his forebear, Prophet Muḥammad, is the last *chosen one*. Rather, his spirit, attributes and actions serve as reaffirmations of Prophet Muḥammad's blessed sowing and reminders of God's *guardianship* through a *guardian*.

The 4th Guardian: Reminding Through Worship

It has been reported that Muḥammad ibn Idrīs al-Shāfiʿī (d. 204 AH), father of the *Shāfiʿī* school of jurisprudence, described the 4th Imam[161] as one of superior knowledge. As accounted by al-Jāḥiẓ (d. 255 AH),

وقال الشافعي في الرسالة في إثبات خبر الواحد:
وجدت علي بن الحسين – وهو أفقه أهل المدينة –
يعول على أخبار الآحاد.

In the treatise dealing with[162] establishing [the reliability] of khabar al-wāḥid[163], al-Shāfiʿī said, "I have found that ʿAlī[164] son of Ḥusayn[165] – who is the most knowledgeable[166] among the people of Madīnah – relies on akhbār al-āḥād[167].[168]

The significance of this quote, for our purposes here, resides not in whether the 4th *guardian* relied on *akhbār al-āḥād* and what exactly that means. That is a debate reserved for the corridors of expertise by scholars of jurisprudence. Rather, the moral of this story is al-Shāfiʿī's passing salute to the 4th Imam's outstanding erudition.

Due to an ailment[169], the 4th *guardian* had survived the massacre at Karbalāʾ[170] of 61 AH, on the day of ʿĀshūrāʾ[171], in which the 3rd *guardian* and the grossly outnumbered supporters of his cause made a sacrificial stand for justice. ʿAlī son of

Ḥusayn, the 4th Imam, lived on to carry the torch in the aftermath. The Umayyads were still in power and, after shedding the blood of Ḥusayn – the last *chosen one's* flesh and blood[172] – what red lines would they not cross? The 4th *guardian* navigated the lethal waters with an eye to the future of the *guarded community*. He embodied the spirit of devotion to *the one with no need*, nurtured a rightly-guided community that could stand the test of time, and wisely maneuvered through the political scene in ways that continue to be analyzed.

In his *Tārīkh Madīnat Dimashq*, the historian Ibn ʿAsākir (d. 571 AH) reports that Mālik ibn Anas (d. 179 AH) said,

> [...] ولقد بلغني أنه كان يصلي في كل يوم وليلة ألف ركعة إلى أن مات وكان يسمى بالمدينة زين العابدين لعبادته.
>
> *[...] And [news] has reached me that [ʿAlī son of Ḥusayn] used to pray one thousand [units of prayer][173] in every day and night [of his life] until he died; and, in Madīnah,*

he was called "the finest of those who worship [God]"[174] because of his worship.[175]

This distinct devotion is not to be understood as merely an expression of dedication. Granted, that would be commendable, but this is much more. In light of the 4th *guardian's* spiritual heritage and life struggles, the manifestation of such exceptional piety speaks to a heart beaming with intense awareness, iron will-power, and Divinely-inspired stamina. The 4th Imam is also referred to by another title in the same spirit, "the one of frequent prostration."[176]

Another historian, also outside the *guarded community*, sums up what many others have said and continue to say about the 4th Imam. In the words of Ibn Khallikān (d. 681 AH),

وفضائل زين العابدين ومناقبه أكثر من أن تحصر.

The merits and virtues of Zayn al-ʿĀbidīn [the finest of those who worship][177] are too many to count.[178]

The 3rd Guardian: Subsisting After Existing

Within and outside the *guarded community,* generations have passed down reports that can be traced back to the last *chosen one,* Prophet Muḥammad. The content in the bulk of these transmitted traditions converges strikingly when it comes to the status of the 3rd, 2nd and 1st *guardians* following Prophet Muḥammad. Similar to how much of the common Muslim heritage confirms the notion of "12 Successors[179]" prophesied by the last *chosen one*, and just as the leading figures discussed thus far are mutually revered inside and outside of the *guarded community*, the earlier Imams are especially so. The challenge this condensed work presents to the reader outside of the *guarded community* is not so much about whether or not these individuals are to be honored reference points – that much is arguably obvious. Instead, the questions this exposition invites contemplation on are: Can this all be a coincidence? Can all the pieces of the puzzle fit so aptly and yet leave us room to doubt whether these individuals are the rightful successors to the last *chosen one*? If we anticipate that the All-Wise would appoint impeccable *guardians*, then who would be more suited for the role than the unmatched series of leaders discussed here?

A compiler of one of the influential tradition collections outside the *guarded community*, Muḥammad ibn ʿĪsá al-Tirmidhī (d. 279 AH), relays that the last *chosen one* said,

حسين مني وأنا من حسين، أحب الله من أحب حسينا، حسين سبط من الأسباط.

> *Ḥusayn*[180] *is from me and I am from Ḥusayn; God loves the one who loves Ḥusayn; Ḥusayn is a sibṭ*[181] *among al-asbāṭ*[182].[183]

It might seem like a straightforward statement at first. Ḥusayn is the grandson of Muḥammad and so it makes sense that, "Ḥusayn is from" Muḥammad's flesh and blood. But how is Muḥammad from Ḥusayn? I will not claim to interpret the depth of meaning potentially entailed here. The reader might be tempted to consider the relationship between the *existence* of the last "software" update at the hands of Prophet Muḥammad and the *subsistence* of that message through the sacrifice of Imam Ḥusayn on the day of ʿĀshūrāʾ... According to the next phrase in the quote above, *the one with no need* has made the love of Ḥusayn a moral compass of sorts. God has special compassion in store for hearts that burn with the love of Ḥusayn. Truly loving Ḥusayn is naturally connected to following the last *chosen one*. The Qurʾān invites us when addressing the last *chosen one*,

قُل إِن كُنتُم تُحِبّونَ اللَّهَ فَاتَّبِعوني يُحبِبكُمُ اللَّهُ وَيَغفِر لَكُم ذُنوبَكُم ۗ وَاللَّهُ غَفورٌ رَحيمٌ

Say, 'If you love God, then follow me; God will love you and forgive you your sins, and God is all-forgiving, all-merciful.'[184]

The final phrase in the quote describes Imam Ḥusayn as a *sibṭ* among a group of other *asbāṭ*.[185] The cross-referencing of this term with Qur'ānic usage[186] of the word[187] can offer insights into the distinguished status Prophet Muḥammad is declaring Imam Ḥusayn to have.[188]

Aḥmad ibn Ḥanbal (d. 241 AH), father of the Ḥanbalī school of jurisprudence, reports that the last *chosen one* said,

[...]فاستأذن ربه ان يسلم علي ويبشرني ان الحسن والحسين سيدا شباب أهل الجنة وان فاطمة سيدة نساء أهل الجنة [...]

[...The angel...] requested permission from His Lord to greet me with peace and give

> *me glad tidings that Ḥasan[189] and Ḥusayn[190] are the leaders[191] of paradise's youth and that Fāṭimah[192] is the leader of paradise's women [...]*[193]

Ḥusayn and his older brother Ḥasan are leaders, Imams, with authority over the youth of paradise (presumably, the people of paradise can enjoy their heart's desire of eternal youth). Who is more qualified to be the *guardian* of the final prescription of excellence for humanity – someone guaranteed to be the authority in paradise or someone who is not? I rest my case. Who is the anticipated successor of the last *chosen one,* appointed by God, for all affairs – worldly and otherworldly? The answer is right before our eyes as well as in between the lines. Lady Fāṭimah is at the center. Look to her father, the last of the *chosen ones*. Look to her husband, the 1st of the *guardians*. Then come eleven Imams – her sons and grandsons.

The 2nd Guardian: Enjoying the Love of the Most Beloved

He was the son of the 1st *guardian,* but the very first *guardian* among the *descendants* of Prophet Muḥammad through Muḥammad's daughter, Lady Fāṭimah. The 2nd *guardian*[194] benefitted from the best role models and confronted treacherous enemies. Patience, generosity and wisdom characterize his legacy. Perhaps these are some reasons why *the one with no need* made him so beloved.

Muslim ibn al-Ḥajjāj (d. 261 AH), one of the authoritative compilers of traditions outside the *guarded community,* reports that Prophet Muḥammad said the following about the 2nd *guardian,*

[...] اللهم إني أحبه فأحبه وأحبب من يحبه

> *[...] O God, indeed I love him, so love him and love the one who loves him.*[195]

This is by no means an ordinary display of affection. As the Qur᾽ān puts it, describing the last *chosen one,*

ما ضَلَّ صاحِبُكُم وَما غَوىٰ. وَما يَنطِقُ عَنِ الهَوىٰ. إن هُوَ إلّا وَحيٌ يوحىٰ

> *[...] has neither gone astray, nor gone amiss. Nor does he speak out of [his own] desire: it is just a revelation that is revealed [to him]*[196]

So when Prophet Muḥammad verifiably loves the 2nd Imam, it is sanctified love. When the last *chosen one* prays that God love the 2nd *guardian*, it is a level of sacred praise. But he goes beyond this when he prays, "and love the one who loves him." The 2nd *guardian* is of such a status that loving him invites Divine love. I do not claim to interpret the layers of meaning here – there is enough light in the room to realize that we are only scratching the surface. Is this just any degree of love? How powerful is this passion? What can make love so impactful? These are thoughts for each reader to reflect on.

A chief authority outside the *guarded community* when it comes to tradition transmission, al-Ḥākim al-Naysābūrī (d. 405 AH), reports the reliability of the following words attributed to the last *chosen one*,

الحسن والحسين سيدا شباب أهل الجنة وأبوهما خير منهما

> *Ḥasan*[197] *and Ḥusayn*[198] *are the leaders*[199] *of paradise's youth and their father*[200] *is better than them both.*[201]

Thus, the status of the 2nd and 3rd Imams is indisputable. Imam Ḥasan is a leader of righteousness in the truest sense existence has to offer, and that reality presents itself in the realm of paradise. Is the realm of paradise, the hereafter, disconnected from this world? Would not the ideal world of this life be led by the rightful leaders of the hereafter's paradise? The reader has, perhaps, known this all along. Imam Ḥasan – in all his greatness – is such a leader. So what have you of his physical and spiritual ancestor who is greater yet? The 1st *guardian* was the immediate protégé and disciple of the last *chosen one*. The *guarded community* is forever defined by his radiant sun.

The 1st Guardian: Guarding the Qurʾān

According to Muslim ibn al-Ḥajjāj (d. 261 AH), in addition to several other compilers of authoritative tradition collections outside the *guarded community*, the last *chosen one* explicitly described the station of our 1st *guardian*[202] saying,

[...] أنت مني بمنزلة هارون من موسى الا انه لا نبي بعدي

[...O ʿAlī] You are to me as Aaron[203] was to Moses[204], except that there is no prophet after me.[205]

There is no confusion on the latter phrase, for the Qurʾān states that Prophet Muḥammad is the "Seal of the Prophets (*khātam al-nabiyyīn*)."[206] The words of the last *chosen one* confirm this Qurʾānic statement. Besides this, the 1st Imam is the true inheritor of the last *chosen one*, just as Aaron was to Moses. As for the position of Aaron to Moses, the Qurʾānic account of their relationship would have been readily summoned in the minds of those who committed the Qurʾān to memory or at least recited it with devotion. For example, the Qurʾān says,

وَلَقَدْ آتَيْنا موسَى الكِتابَ وَجَعَلنا مَعَهُ أَخاهُ هارونَ وَزيرًا

Certainly We gave Moses the Book and We made Aaron, his brother, accompany him as a minister.[207]

The Qurʾān also quotes Moses telling Aaron the following,

[...] وَقالَ موسىٰ لِأَخيهِ هارونَ اخلُفني في قَومي [...]

[...] And Moses said to Aaron, his brother, 'Be my successor among my people [...][208]

There are many other verses related to this as well. Yet, are not these two verses alone telling enough? What more informative of an analogy could be employed to emphasize that ʿAlī ibn Abī Ṭālib is the 1st *guardian*, the successor to the last *chosen one*?

Al-Ḥākim al-Naysābūrī (d. 405 AH) reports that the last *chosen one* said,

[...] علي مع القرآن والقرآن مع علي لن يتفرقا حتى يردا على الحوض

[...] ʿAlī is with the Qurʾān and the Qurʾān is with ʿAlī; they will never separate [from one another] until they meet [me] at the ḥawḍ[209].[210]

Just as the Qurʾān is impeccable so is ʿAlī. Neither does he deviate from it nor does it ever lead away from him. There are countless other indications – some perhaps of a greater priority than the ones mentioned here – that the 1st *guardian* has an unparalleled station of knowledge, spirituality and authority to lead. However, the scarce references made here to Imam ʿAlī's merits, as well as to those of the remaining 11 Imams, can give a taste of pure guidance and a glimpse of light in the darkness.

NOTES

[1] References are particularly due to lectures and works by:

- S. Muḥammad Ḥusayn al-Ṭabāṭabā'ī
- Sh. Murtaḍá al-Muṭahharī
- S. Muḥammad Bāqir al-Ṣadr
- Sh. Ghulām Riḍā al-Fayyāḍī
- Sh. Nāṣir Makārim al-Shīrāzī
- Sh. Ja'far al-Subḥānī
- S. Ja'far al-Ḥakīm
- S. Munīr al-Khabbāz
- S. Muḥammad Bāqir al-Sīstānī
- S. Muḥammad 'Alī Baḥr al-'ulūm
- S. Sāmī al-Badrī
- S. Ja'far Murtaḍá al-'Āmilī
- S. Muḥammad Rizvī

[2] Attributed to 'Alī ibn al-Ḥusayn, known as Zayn al-'ābidīn, Munājāt al-Shākirīn

[3] See the previous booklets in this series

[4] Miracles, on the other hand, are exceptions to the norm and occur as Divine Wisdom deems appropriate; they are not meant to defeat the purpose of life as a test and opportunity for humans to paint their true colors.

[5] For example, in this age of the 12th Imam's hidden identity, the upright expert scholars are reference points that non-experts refer to for their practical questions on religious life. This is despite the fact that these experts disagree at times and do not claim to be infallible in their conclusions. But the existence of the 12th Imam, a living immaculate and a physical conduit expressing God's will constantly, can sanction the framework of referring to these experts. The Imam exists as a living role model with all the correct answers, ready to lead on all levels, and as a physical guarantor that the threshold of guidance is available to seekers of truth.

[6] For searchable references both within and without the *guarded community*, see Sh. al-Ṣāfī al-Gulpaygānī's *Muntakhab al-Athar*, published online through *Markaz al-Dirāsāt al-Takhaṣṣuṣiyyah Fī al-Imām al-Mahdī (ʿaj)*.

There are 148 reports referring to the "12" successors of the last *chosen one*, the same number as the 12 chiefs (*nuqabāʾ*) of the Israelites and the 12 disciples of Jesus, peace be upon him. Another 161 reports give additional descriptions of these 12 successors.

Luṭf Allāh Al-Ṣāfī al-Gulpaygānī, *Muntakhab al-Athar Fī al-Imām al-Thānī ʿAshar ʿAlayh al-Salām*, 1st ed., vol. 1-3 (Qom: Maktabat Āyat Allāh al-ʿUẓmá al-Ṣāfī al-Gulpaygānī, Waḥdat al-Nashr al-ʿĀlamiyyah, 1422 AH), May 19, 2013, accessed June 3, 2017,
http://www.m-mahdi.net/main/books-120
http://www.m-mahdi.net/main/books-121
http://www.m-mahdi.net/main/books-122

[7] See S. Sāmī al-Badrī's work on 5 Methodologies for establishing the Imāmah of Ahl al-Bayt, peace be upon them; the second methodology: through the holy books recognized by Jews and Christians.

Sāmī Al-Badrī, *Manāhij Khamsah Fī al-Istidlāl ʿAlá Imāmat Ahl al-Bayt (ʿa)*, 1st ed. (Baghdad: Dār Ṭūr Sīnīn lil-Ṭibāʿah wa al-Nashr, 1421 AH / 2000 CE), http://al-badri.info/books/emameh5/index.htm.

[8] 12th Imam: Muḥammad son of Ḥasan (b. 255 AH)

Muḥammad Ḥusayn Al-Ḥusaynī al-Jalālī, *Fihris al-Turāth*, ed. Muḥammad Jawād Al-Ḥusaynī Al-Jalālī, 1st ed., vol. 1 (Qom: Dalīl Mā, 1422 AH), Ahlulbayt Library 2.0, 283; Muḥammad ibn Muḥammad ibn al-Nuʿmān al-Mufīd (d. 413 AH), *al-Irshād*, 2nd ed., vol. 2 (Beirut: Dār al-Mufīd lil-Ṭibāʿah wa al-Nashr wa al-Tawzīʿ, 1414 AH / 1993 CE), Ahlulbayt Library 2.0, 339.

[9] Qurʾān 5:110

إذ قالَ اللَّهُ يا عيسَى ابنَ مَريَمَ اذكُر نِعمَتي عَلَيكَ وَعَلىٰ والِدَتِكَ إذ أيَّدتُكَ بِروحِ القُدُسِ تُكَلِّمُ النّاسَ فِي المَهدِ وَكَهلًا ۖ وَإذ عَلَّمتُكَ الكِتابَ وَالحِكمَةَ وَالتَّوراةَ وَالإنجيلَ ۖ وَإذ تَخلُقُ مِنَ الطّينِ كَهَيئَةِ الطَّيرِ بِإذني فَتَنفُخُ فيها فَتَكونُ طَيرًا بِإذني ۖ وَتُبرِئُ الأَكمَهَ وَالأَبرَصَ بِإذني ۖ وَإذ تُخرِجُ المَوتىٰ بِإذني ۖ وَإذ كَفَفتُ بَني إسرائيلَ عَنكَ إذ جِئتَهُم بِالبَيِّناتِ فَقالَ الَّذينَ كَفَروا مِنهُم إن هٰذا إلّا سِحرٌ مُبينٌ

When God will say, O Jesus son of Mary, remember My blessing upon you and upon your mother, when I strengthened you with the Holy Spirit, so you would speak to the people in the cradle and in adulthood, and when I taught you the Book and wisdom, the Torah and the Evangel, and when you would create from clay the form of a bird, with My leave, and you would breathe into it and it would become a bird, with My leave; and you would heal the blind and the leper, with My leave, and you would raise the dead, with My leave; and when I held off [the evil of] the Children of Israel from you when you brought them manifest proofs, whereat the faithless among them said, 'This is nothing but plain magic.'

[10] Qur'ān 29:14

وَلَقَد أَرسَلنا نوحًا إلىٰ قَومِهِ فَلَبِثَ فيهِم أَلفَ سَنَةٍ إلّا خَمسينَ عامًا فَأَخَذَهُمُ الطّوفانُ وَهُم ظالِمونَ

Certainly We sent Noah to his people, and he remained with them for a thousand years, less fifty. Then the flood overtook them while they were wrongdoers.

[11] Qur'ān 12:58

وَجاءَ إِخوَةُ يوسُفَ فَدَخَلوا عَلَيهِ فَعَرَفَهُم وَهُم لَهُ مُنكِرونَ

[After some years] the brothers of Joseph came and entered his presence. He recognized them, but they did not recognize him.

12 See previous reference to *Muntakhab al-Athar*. An example of a much earlier compilation of related reports can be found in *Kifāyat al-Athar* by al-Khazzāz al-Qummī (d. ca late 4th century AH).

13 There are dozens of other non-Shīʿī testimonies. For additional references, follow compiled lists in these representative works:

Thāmir Al-ʿAmīdī, *Difāʿ ʿAn al-Kāfī*, 1st ed., vol. 1-2 (Markaz al-Ghadīr lil-Dirāsāt al-Islāmiyyah, 1415 AH), PDF;

Ḥusayn al-Nūrī al-Ṭabarsī (d. 1320 AH), *Kashf al-Astār ʿAn Wajh al-Ghāʾib ʿAn al-Abṣār*, 2nd ed. (Qom: Maṭbaʿat al-Khiyām, 1400 AH), PDF;

Luṭf Allāh al-Ṣāfī al-Gulpaygānī, *Muntakhab al-Athar Fī al-Imām al-Thānī ʿAshar ʿAlayh al-Salām*, 1st ed., vol. 2 (Qom: Maktabat Āyat Allāh al-ʿUẓmá al-Ṣāfī al-Gulpaygānī, Waḥdat al-Nashr al-ʿĀlamiyyah, 1422 AH), May 19, 2013, accessed June 3, 2017, http://www.m-mahdi.net/main/books-121;

Al-Raḥmah, Ḥikmat. *Aʾimmah Ahl al-Bayt ʿalayhim al-Salām fī Kutub Ahl al-Sunnah*. Qom: Muʾassasat al-Kawthar lil-Maʿārif al-Islāmiyyah. Electronic.

This last reference includes testimonies for the remaining *guardians*/Imams as well.

[14] The dates in this booklet are listed in reference to the lunar *hijrī* calendar; starting "after the hijrah (migration)" (AH) of the last *chosen one*, Prophet Muḥammad, from Mecca to Medina. Conversion from *hijrī* to Gregorian dates has a level of uncertainty due to limited information and different theories about how to establish the beginning of a lunar calendar month. In addition, many interested readers may find it more convenient to keep track of dates in Islamic history based on the lunar *hijrī* calendar, in line with the convention of the primary sources referenced.

[15] The 11th Imam

[16] The 10th Imam

[17] *Imām*; likely used in this instance to mean leader more generally, not impeccable *guardian*. The word *Imām* can be used in many different senses. For example, it can refer to one who leads congregational prayers, a community leader, or a towering scholarly figure.

[18] Abū al-Khayr Shams al-Dīn Muḥammad Al-Jazarī (d. 833 AH), *Asná al-Maṭālib fī Manāqib Sayyidinā ʿAlī ibn Abī Ṭālib*, ed. Muḥammad Hādī Al-Amīnī (Isfahān: Maktabat al-Imām Amīr al-Muʾminīn ʿalayh al-Salām al-ʿĀmmah), Electronic, 86-87.

[19] Often called *al-ghaybah al-ṣughrá*, variably translated as, "the minor occultation"

[20] Often called *al-ghaybah al-kubrá,* variably translated as, "the major occultation"

[21] *ḥawādith*

[22] *irjiʿū*

[23] Although the Arabic only uses the word *ruwāt* (transmitters), these are obviously meant to be the transmitters who properly understand the reports in a holistic fashion; those who would be referred to today as the specialists, the experts, the reference points who have proper justifications for their understanding of the heritage passed down, generation after generation, since the last *chosen one.* These experts are called the *marājʿ* (sing. *marjiʿ*) – "the ones referred to"; they are the leading *mujtahidūn* (sing. *mujtahid*) – the experts capable of deducing legal rulings from the original source material: namely, the Qurʾān, the *Sunnah* (Prophetic tradition as safeguarded by the 12 immaculate Imams)... *Mujtahidūn* are predominantly trained and recognized after long years of rigorous study and religious practice in contemporary Twelver Shīʿī centers/communities of learning (classically referred to as *al-ḥawzah al-ʿilmiyyah* or *ḥawzah,* for short; the Islamic seminary). In today's Twelver Shīʿī world, the title "Āyatullāh" is arguably intended to signify someone who has been recognized as a *mujtahid,* while the title "Āyatullāh al-ʿUẓmá" signifies someone who has become widely recognized not only as a *mujtahid* but as a fully

qualified reference point who people actively refer to. In matters that are not already known to an individual, a non-expert member of the *guarded community* is expected to either take precaution in practice or refer to a leading *mujtahid*. Generally speaking, if the leading *mujtahidūn* disagree on something, the non-expert is initially only excused to refer to the most learned living *mujtahid* among the leading *mujtahidūn*. If, however, the most learned living *mujtahid* has research findings that excuse reference to any other *mujtahid*, then the non-expert becomes excused to refer to other *mujtahidūn* as well.

24 *ruwāt*

25 *ḥadīth*

26 *ḥujjah*

27 *ḥujjah*

28 Abū Jaʿfar Muḥammad ibn ʿAlī ibn al-Ḥusayn ibn Bābawayh al-Qummī al-Ṣadūq (d. 381 AH), *Kamāl al-Dīn wa Tamām al-Niʿmah*, ed. ʿAlī Akbar Al-Ghaffārī (Qom: Muʾassasat al-Nashr al-Islāmī, 1405 AH), Ahlulbayt Library 2.0, 484.

29 See next section

30 Many individuals

31 The Shīʿī community that followed this specific line of *guardians*

32 *Al-Amr*; the authority; the command; a reference to the Imam position of *guardian*

[33] 11th Imam: Ḥasan son of ʿAlī (232 AH – 260 AH)
Muḥammad ibn Muḥammad ibn al-Nuʿmān al-Mufīd (d. 413 AH), *al-Irshād*, 2nd ed., vol. 2 (Beirut: Dār al-Mufīd lil-Ṭibāʿah wa al-Nashr wa al-Tawzīʿ, 1414 AH / 1993 CE), Ahlulbayt Library 2.0, 313.

[34] The Shīʿī community that followed this specific line of *guardians*

[35] The *ghaybah*; variably translated as occultation, absence, hiding, concealment, hidden identity, living incognito, etc...

[36] Abū al-Ḥasan ʿAlī ibn al-Ḥusayn Al-Masʿūdī (d. ca 345 AH), *Ithbāt al-Waṣiyyah*, 2nd ed. (Beirut: Dār al-Aḍwāʾ lil-Ṭibāʿah wa al-Nashr wa al-Tawzīʿ, 1988 CE / 1409 AH), PDF, 286.

[37] Six years
Muḥammad ibn Muḥammad ibn al-Nuʿmān al-Mufīd (d. 413 AH), *al-Irshād*, 2nd ed., vol. 2 (Beirut: Dār al-Mufīd lil-Ṭibāʿah wa al-Nashr wa al-Tawzīʿ, 1414 AH / 1993 CE), Ahlulbayt Library 2.0, 313.

[38] *ʿulamāʾ* (sing. *ʿālim*); knowledgeable ones, scholars, etc.

[39] The 11th Imam

[40] The 10th Imam

[41] The 9th Imam

[42] The 8th Imam

[43] The 7th Imam

[44] The 6th Imam

[45] The 5th Imam

[46] The 4th Imam

[47] The 3rd Imam

[48] The 1st Imam; the 2nd Imam is not mentioned in this lineage because he is the brother of the 3rd Imam

[49] *Al-ʿAjam*; foreigners; can also refer specifically to Persians

[50] ʿAmr Ibn Baḥr al-Jāḥiẓ (d. 255 AH), *Rasāʾil al-Jāḥiẓ*, comp. Ḥasan Al-Sindūbī, 1st ed. (Al-Maktabah al-Tijāriyyah al-Kubrá, 1933 CE / 1352 AH), 109, accessed June 5, 2017, Bibliotheca Alexandrina, keyword: http://dar.bibalex.org/webpages/dar.jsf.

[51] *ʿālim*; knowledgeable one, scholar, etc.

[52] Yūsuf ibn ʿAbd Allāh Sibṭ ibn al-Jawzī (d. 654 AH), *Tadhkirat al-Khawāṣ* (Tehran: Maktabat Nīnawá al-Ḥadīthah), PDF, 362.

[53] 10th Imam: ʿAlī son of Muḥammad (212 AH – 254 AH) Muḥammad ibn Muḥammad ibn al-Nuʿmān al-Mufīd (d. 413 AH), *al-Irshād*, 2nd ed., vol. 2 (Beirut: Dār al-Mufīd lil-Ṭibāʿah wa al-Nashr wa al-Tawzīʿ, 1414 AH / 1993 CE), Ahlulbayt Library 2.0, 297.

[54] Muḥammad ibn Muḥammad ibn al-Nuʿmān al-Mufīd (d. 413 AH), *al-Irshād*, 2nd ed., vol. 2 (Beirut: Dār al-Mufīd lil-Ṭibāʿah wa al-Nashr wa al-Tawzīʿ, 1414 AH / 1993 CE), Ahlulbayt Library 2.0, 309.

[55] That is, Muḥammad son of Ḥasan (the 12th Imam)

[56] Shihāb al-Dīn Yāqūt Al-Ḥamawī (d. 626 AH), *Muʿjam al-Buldān*, vol. 4 (Beirut: Dār Iḥyāʾ al-Turāth al-ʿArabī, 1979 CE / 1399 AH), Ahlulbayt Library 2.0, 123.

[57] The 10th Imam's *kunyah*, or epithet

[58] The 10th Imam

[59] *Al-Jawād*

[60] The 9th Imam

[61] This is likely *al-Riḍá* (*al-Riḍā*) because that is the commonly known description of the 8th Imam, but may be *al-Raḍīyy* if the last Arabic letter (ى) is missing dots in the manuscript (ي); regardless, the root of this word relates to satisfaction, being pleased and content; among the possible meanings, this word could be referring to someone's favorable regard for the Imam (e.g. God being pleased with him), the Imam's contentment with another (e.g. the Imam being content with God's decrees), or the Imam's pleasing nature (e.g. the Imam being pleasing to God or the righteous)

[62] The 8th Imam

[63] *Al-Kāẓim*; the one who holds back his anger

[64] The 7th Imam

[65] Al-Ṣādiq

[66] The 6th Imam

[67] The 3rd Imam

[68] The 1st Imam

[69] The 10th Imam

[70] *Al-Hādī*

[71] This appears to be an approximate age, unless it is based on the alternative possibility of the 10th Imam's year of birth, 214 AH, as in:
Abū Ja'far Muḥammad ibn Ya'qūb al-Kulaynī (d. ca 329 AH / 941 CE), *al-Kāfī*, ed. 'Alī Akbar al-Ghafārī, 4th ed., vol. 1 (Tehran: Dār al-Kutub al-Islāmīyah, 1984 CE), Ahlulbayt Library 2.0, 497.

[72] *Faqīh*; erudite sage, scholar, jurist, etc...

[73] *Imām*; used in this instance to mean leader more generally, not impeccable *guardian*. The word *Imām* can be used in many different senses. For example, it can refer to one who leads congregational prayers, a community leader, or a towering scholarly figure.

[74] *Muta'abbid*

[75] Shams al-Dīn Muḥammad ibn Aḥmad Al-Dhahabī (d. 748 AH), *al-'Ibar Fī Khabar Man Ghabar*, ed. Muḥammad Al-Sa'īd Zaghlūl, vol. 1 (Beirut: Dār al-Kutub al-'Ilmiyyah, 1985 CE / 1405 AH), PDF, 364.

[76] *Ahl al-Bayt*; the household of Muḥammad, the Seal of All Prophets, the last *chosen one*

[77] 9th Imam: Muḥammad son of 'Alī (195 AH – 220 AH)
Muḥammad ibn Muḥammad ibn al-Nu'mān al-Mufīd (d. 413 AH), *al-Irshād*, 2nd ed., vol. 2 (Beirut: Dār al-Mufīd lil-Ṭibā'ah wa al-Nashr wa al-Tawzī', 1414 AH / 1993 CE), Ahlulbayt Library 2.0, 273.

[78] Qurʾān 19:29-34

فَأَشارَت إِلَيهِ ۖ قالوا كَيفَ نُكَلِّمُ مَن كانَ فِي المَهدِ صَبِيًّا

قالَ إِنّي عَبدُ اللَّهِ آتانِيَ الكِتابَ وَجَعَلَني نَبِيًّا

وَجَعَلَني مُبارَكًا أَينَ ما كُنتُ وَأَوصاني بِالصَّلاةِ وَالزَّكاةِ ما دُمتُ حَيًّا

وَبَرًّا بِوالِدَتي وَلَم يَجعَلني جَبّارًا شَقِيًّا

وَالسَّلامُ عَلَيَّ يَومَ وُلِدتُ وَيَومَ أَموتُ وَيَومَ أُبعَثُ حَيًّا

Thereat she pointed to him. They said, 'How can we speak to one who is yet a baby in the cradle?'
He said, 'Indeed I am a servant of God! He has given me the Book and made me a prophet.
He has made me blessed, wherever I may be, and He has enjoined me to [maintain] the prayer and to [pay] the zakāt *as long as I live,*
and to be good to my mother, and He has not made me self-willed and wretched.
Peace is to me the day I was born, and the day I die, and the day I am raised alive.'

[79] Shams al-Dīn Muḥammad ibn Aḥmad Al-Dhahabī (d. 748 AH), *Tārīkh al-Islām*, ed. ʿUmar ʿAbd Al-Salām Tudmurī, 1st ed., vol. 15 (Beirut: Dār al-Kitāb al-ʿArabī, 1987 CE / 1407 AH), Ahlulbayt Library 2.0, 385.

[80] Muḥammad ibn Ṭalḥah Al-Shāfiʿī (d. 652 AH), *Maṭālib al-Saʾūl Fī Manāqib Āl al-Rasūl*, ed. Mājid Aḥmad Al-ʿAṭiyyah, vol. 1, Ahlulbayt Library 2.0, 467.

[81] Ibn al-Ṣabbāgh Al-Mālikī (d. 855 AH), *Al-Fuṣūl al-Muhimmah Fī Maʿrifat al-Aʾimmah*, ed. Sāmī Al-Gharīrī, 1st

ed., vol. 2 (Qom: Dār al-Ḥadīth lil-Ṭibāʿah wa al-Nashr, 1422 AH), Ahlulbayt Library 2.0, 1035.

82 Qurʾān 9:32

يُرِيدُونَ أَن يُطْفِئُوا نُورَ اللَّهِ بِأَفْوَاهِهِمْ وَيَأْبَى اللَّهُ إِلَّا أَن يُتِمَّ نُورَهُ وَلَوْ كَرِهَ الْكَافِرُونَ

> *They desire to put out the light of God with their mouths, but God is intent on perfecting His light though the faithless should be averse.*

83 Yūsuf ibn ʿAbd Allāh Sibṭ ibn al-Jawzī (d. 654 AH), *Tadhkirat al-Khawāṣ* (Tehran: Maktabat Nīnawá al-Ḥadīthah), PDF, 358-359.

84 8th Imam: ʿAlī son of Mūsá (148 AH – 203 AH) Muḥammad ibn Muḥammad ibn al-Nuʿmān al-Mufīd (d. 413 AH), *al-Irshād*, 2nd ed., vol. 2 (Beirut: Dār al-Mufīd lil-Ṭibāʿah wa al-Nashr wa al-Tawzīʿ, 1414 AH / 1993 CE), Ahlulbayt Library 2.0, 247.

85 The 8th Imam

86 *ḥadīth*

87 The 7th Imam

88 *yuftī*

89 Muḥammad

90 May God shower peace and blessings upon him [and his progeny]

91 Yūsuf ibn ʿAbd Allāh Sibṭ ibn al-Jawzī (d. 654 AH), *Tadhkirat al-Khawāṣ* (Tehran: Maktabat Nīnawá al-Ḥadīthah), PDF, 351-352.

92 *akhlāq*

93 ʿAbd al-Ḥamīd ibn Abī al-Ḥadīd (d. 656 AH), *Sharḥ Nahj al-Balāghah*, ed. Muḥammad Abū Al-Faḍl Ibrāhīm, 1st ed., vol. 15 (Dār Iḥyāʾ al-Kutub al-ʿArabiyyah, 1378 AH / 1959 CE), Ahlulbayt Library 2.0, 291.

94 At least if a single authority must exist in certain cases and taking precaution is not an option

95 *Ahl al-Bayt*

96 Sing. *Hāshimī*; belonging to the clan whose lineage is traced back to Hāshim, the great grandfather of Muḥammad

97 The 8th Imam; *al-Riḍā*

98 In northeastern Iran

99 Al-Maʾmūn: ʿAbd Allāh ibn Hārūn al-Rashīd (d. 218 AH)

100 In present-day Mashhad, Iran.

101 Al-Rashīd: Hārūn ibn Muḥammad al-Mahdī (d. 193 AH); father of al-Maʾmūn

102 *Al-Riḍā*

103 *Al-Muṣtafá*; the *chosen one*, the Prophet Muḥammad

104 *Ahl al-Bayt*

105 Muḥammad Ibn Ḥibbān (d. 354 AH), *Al-Thuqāt*, 1st ed., vol. 8 (Hyderabad Deccan: Dāʾirat al-Maʿārif al-ʿUthmāniyyah, 1982 CE / 1402 AH), Ahlulbayt Library 2.0, 456-457.

106 Muḥammad Ibn Ḥibbān (d. 354 AH), *Al-Thuqāt*, 1st ed., vol. 8 (Hyderabad Deccan: Dāʾirat al-Maʿārif al-

ʿUthmāniyyah, 1982 CE / 1402 AH), Ahlulbayt Library 2.0, 456.

[107] See previous booklets in this series.

[108] 7th Imam: Mūsá son of Jaʿfar (128 AH – 183 AH) Muḥammad ibn Muḥammad ibn al-Nuʿmān al-Mufīd (d. 413 AH), *al-Irshād*, 2nd ed., vol. 2 (Beirut: Dār al-Mufīd lil-Ṭibāʿah wa al-Nashr wa al-Tawzīʿ, 1414 AH / 1993 CE), Ahlulbayt Library 2.0, 215.

[109] *Imām*; used in this instance to mean leader more generally, not impeccable *guardian*. The word *Imām* can be used in many different senses. For example, it can refer to one who leads congregational prayers, a community leader, or a towering scholarly figure.

[110] ʿAbd al-Raḥmān Ibn Abī Ḥātim al-Rāzī (d. 327 AH), *Al-Jarḥ wa al-Taʿdīl*, 1st ed., vol. 8 (Beirut: Dār Iḥyāʾ al-Turāth al-ʿArabī, 1953 CE / 1372 AH), Ahlulbayt Library 2.0, 139.

[111] *Al-Bāqir*; a reference to the 5th Imam

[112] *Al-Ṣādiq*; a reference to the 6th Imam

[113] *Al-Kāẓim*; the one who holds back his anger; a reference to the 7th Imam

[114] *Al-Riḍā*; a reference to the 8th Imam

[115] Muḥammad ibn ʿUmar Fakhr al-Dīn al-Rāzī (d. 606 AH), *Tafsīr al-Rāzī*, 3rd ed., vol. 32, Ahlulbayt Library 2.0, 124.

[116] The 6th Imam

[117] *Al-ʿabd al-ṣāliḥ*

[118] Performed *sujūd*

[119] *Taqwá*; God-consciousness; God-wariness; piety

[120] Aḥmad ibn ʿAlī al-Khaṭīb al-Baghdādī (d. 463 AH), *Tārīkh Baghdād*, ed. Muṣṭafá ʿAbd Al-Qādir ʿAṭā, 1st ed., vol. 13 (Beirut: Dār al-Kutub al-ʿIlmiyyah, 1997 CE / 1417 AH), Ahlulbayt Library 2.0, 29.

[121] *Al-Kāẓim*

[122] Status of closeness to God; for which God answers the prayers of those beseeching God through him; the implication is that this honor is apparent because God answers such prayers

[123] Muḥammad ibn Ṭalḥah Al-Shāfiʿī (d. 652 AH), *Maṭālib al-Saʾūl Fī Manāqib Āl al-Rasūl*, ed. Mājid Aḥmad Al-ʿAṭiyyah, vol. 1, Ahlulbayt Library 2.0, 447.

[124] *Afqah*

[125] 6th Imam: Jaʿfar son of Muḥammad (83 AH – 148 AH) Muḥammad ibn Muḥammad ibn al-Nuʿmān al-Mufīd (d. 413 AH), *al-Irshād*, 2nd ed., vol. 2 (Beirut: Dār al-Mufīd lil-Ṭibāʿah wa al-Nashr wa al-Tawzīʿ, 1414 AH / 1993 CE), Ahlulbayt Library 2.0, 179-180.

[126] The 5th Imam

[127] Abū Aḥmad ʿAbd Allāh ibn ʿUday al-Jurjānī (d. 365 AH), *al-Kāmil Fī Ḍuʿafāʾ al-Rijāl*, ed. Suhayl Zakkār and Yaḥyá Mukhtār Ghazzāwī, 3rd ed., vol. 2 (Beirut: Dār al-Fikr lil-Ṭibāʿah wa al-Nashr wa al-Tawzīʿ, 1998 CE / 1409 AH), 132.

Ṣalāḥ al-Dīn Khalīl ibn Aybak al-Ṣafadī (d. 764 AH), *al-Wāfī bil-Wafiyāt*, ed. Aḥmad al-Arnā'ūt and Turkī Muṣṭafá, vol. 11 (Beirut: Dār Iḥyā' al-Turāth, 2000 CE / 1420 AH), Ahlulbayt Library 2.0, 99.

128 *Al-Ṣādiq*

129 Al-Manṣūr: 'Abd Allāh ibn Muḥammad (d. 158 AH); second 'Abbāsid ruler

130 A city in southern Iraq

131 *Futinū*; tested; seduced; tempted; deceived; misled

132 The 6th Imam

133 The 5th Imam

134 Apparently, in an attempt to stump the Imam.

135 Whose epithet (*kunyah*) was *Abū Ja'far*

136 The 6th Imam

137 *Haybah*; prestige; majesty

138 The epithet of the 6th Imam

139 Seems to be referring to al-Manṣūr

140 The city to which the last *chosen one* migrated and in which he is buried

141 Abū Aḥmad 'Abd Allāh ibn 'Uday al-Jurjānī (d. 365 AH), *al-Kāmil Fī Ḍu'afā' al-Rijāl*, ed. Suhayl Zakkār and Yaḥyá Mukhtār Ghazzāwī, 3rd ed., vol. 2 (Beirut: Dār al-Fikr lil-Ṭibā'ah wa al-Nashr wa al-Tawzī', 1998 CE / 1409 AH), 132.

142 Abū Aḥmad 'Abd Allāh ibn 'Uday al-Jurjānī (d. 365 AH), *al-Kāmil Fī Ḍu'afā' al-Rijāl*, ed. Suhayl Zakkār and Yaḥyá

Mukhtār Ghazzāwī, 3rd ed., vol. 2 (Beirut: Dār al-Fikr lil-Ṭibāʿah wa al-Nashr wa al-Tawzīʿ, 1998 CE / 1409 AH), 132.

143 Muḥammad

144 *Iṣfarr*; literally *turn yellow*; in the sense that reverence for the Prophet would manifest as a seemingly visible change in the Imam's demeanor and/or physiology.

145 Muḥammad

146 Some versions of this report read *ṣāʾim* (fasting) as opposed to *ṣāmit* (silence). Fasting may make more sense in order to include states in which the Imam is teaching, for instance. In any case, perhaps the point is not to be entirely exclusive here but merely to direct attention to salient features of the Imam's behavior – at least in the eyes of Mālik.

147 *ʿulamāʾ* (sing. *ʿālim*); erudite sages, knowledgeable ones, scholars, etc.

148 ʿIyāḍ ibn Mūsá al-Yaḥṣibī (d. 544 AH), *Al-Shifā bi Taʿrīf Ḥuqūq al-Muṣtafá*, vol. 1-2 (Beirut: Dār al-Fikr lil-Ṭibāʿah wa al-Nashr wa al-Tawzīʿ, 1988 CE / 1409 AH), Ahlulbayt Library 2.0, 42.

149 5th Imam: Muḥammad son of ʿAlī (57 AH – 114 AH) Muḥammad ibn Muḥammad ibn al-Nuʿmān al-Mufīd (d. 413 AH), *al-Irshād*, 2nd ed., vol. 2 (Beirut: Dār al-Mufīd lil-Ṭibāʿah wa al-Nashr wa al-Tawzīʿ, 1414 AH / 1993 CE), Ahlulbayt Library 2.0, 158.

[150] The 4th Imam

[151] *al-Bāqir*; the one of breakthroughs; the one who reaches the roots and hidden depths.

[152] *Fuqahā*ʾ (sing. *faqīh*); erudite sages, scholars, jurists, etc...

[153] A geographical region located in the west and southwest of the Arabian peninsula; it includes the cities of Makkah and Madīnah.

[154] *al-Fiqh*; precise, deep understanding of the faith, including jurisprudence related to practice.

[155] ʿAmr ibn Baḥr al-Jāḥiẓ (d. 255 AH), *Rasāʾil al-Jāḥiẓ*, comp. Ḥasan Al-Sindūbī, 1st ed. (Al-Maktabah al-Tijāriyyah al-Kubrá, 1933 CE / 1352 AH), 108, accessed June 5, 2017, Bibliotheca Alexandrina, keyword: http://dar.bibalex.org/webpages/dar.jsf.

[156] Jābir ibn ʿAbd Allāh al-Anṣārī (d. 78 AH); a companion of the last *chosen one*.

[157] ʿAmr ibn Baḥr al-Jāḥiẓ (d. 255 AH), *Rasāʾil al-Jāḥiẓ*, comp. Ḥasan Al-Sindūbī, 1st ed. (Al-Maktabah al-Tijāriyyah al-Kubrá, 1933 CE / 1352 AH), 108, accessed June 5, 2017, Bibliotheca Alexandrina, keyword: http://dar.bibalex.org/webpages/dar.jsf.

[158] The epithet of the 5th Imam

[159] *Al-Nubuwwah*; prophet-hood

[160] Aḥmad ibn ʿAbd Allāh Al-Aṣfahānī (d. 430 AH), *Ḥilyat al-Awliyāʾ wa Ṭabaqāt al-Aṣfiyāʾ*, vol. 3 (Beirut: Dār al-Fikr

lil-Ṭibāʿah wa al-Nashr wa al-Tawzīʿ, 1996 CE / 1416 AH), PDF, 180.

161 4th Imam: ʿAlī son of Ḥusayn (38 AH – 95 AH)

Muḥammad ibn Muḥammad ibn al-Nuʿmān al-Mufīd (d. 413 AH), *al-Irshād*, 2nd ed., vol. 2 (Beirut: Dār al-Mufīd lil-Ṭibāʿah wa al-Nashr wa al-Tawzīʿ, 1414 AH / 1993 CE), Ahlulbayt Library 2.0, 137.

162 Alternatively, "in *the Treatise* (*al-Risālah*), in dealing with [...]."

Apparently, al-Jāḥiẓ had access to a work by al-Shāfiʿī from which he quoted this excerpt. In *al-Mustaṣfá* by al-Ghazālī (d. 505 AH), however, a similar quote is attributed to al-Shāfiʿī about ʿAlī son of Ḥusayn without the phrase describing him as the most knowledgeable. This may have been an edit by al-Ghazālī, by someone else, or a quote from a different work by al-Shāfiʿī. Concurring with the content attributed to al-Shāfiʿī here, Ibn Abī al-Ḥadīd al-Muʿtazilī (d. 656 AH) quotes al-Jāḥiẓ's words verbatim in his *Sharḥ Nahj al-Balāghah*. See:

Muḥammad ibn Muḥammad al-Ghazālī (d. 505 AH), *al-Mustaṣfá fī ʿIlm al-Uṣūl*, ed. Muḥammad ʿAbd al-Salām ʿAbd al-Shāfī (Beirut: Dār al-Kutub al-ʿIlmiyyah, 1996 CE / 1417 AH), Ahlulbayt Library 2.0, 119;

ʿAbd al-Ḥamīd ibn Abī al-Ḥadīd (d. 656 AH), *Sharḥ Nahj al-Balāghah*, ed. Muḥammad Abū Al-Faḍl Ibrāhīm, 1st ed., vol. 15 (Dār Iḥyā' al-Kutub al-'Arabiyyah, 1962 CE), Ahlulbayt Library 2.0, 274.

163 A term referring to a type of report transmission that is discussed in the principles of jurisprudence (*uṣūl al-fiqh*).

164 The 4th Imam

165 The 3rd Imam

166 *Afqah*

167 Sing. *khabar al-wāḥid*

168 'Amr ibn Baḥr al-Jāḥiẓ (d. 255 AH), *Rasā'il al-Jāḥiẓ*, comp. Ḥasan Al-Sindūbī, 1st ed. (Al-Maktabah al-Tijāriyyah al-Kubrá, 1933 CE / 1352 AH), 106, accessed June 5, 2017, Bibliotheca Alexandrina, keyword: http://dar.bibalex.org/webpages/dar.jsf.

169 For an analysis of this ailment/injury, see: Muḥammad Riḍā Al-Ḥusaynī al-Jalālī, *Jihād al-Imām al-Sajjād Zayn al-'Ābidīn 'Alī ibn al-Ḥusayn ibn 'Alī ibn Abī Ṭālib 'Alayhim al-Salām*, 1st ed. (Dār al-Ḥadīth, 1418 AH), PDF, 42-47.

170 Located in present-day Iraq, to the south of Baghdad

171 The 10th day of the lunar month called *Muḥarram*

172 The 3rd *guardian*, Ḥusayn son of 'Alī, was Prophet Muḥammad's grandson.

173 *Rak'ah*

174 *Zayn al-'Ābidīn*

[175] ʿAlī ibn al-Ḥasan ibn Hibat Allāh Ibn ʿAsākir, *Tārīkh Madīnat Dimashq*, ed. ʿAlī Shīrī, 1st ed., vol. 41 (Beirut: Dār al-Fikr lil-Ṭibāʿah wa al-Nashr wa al-Tawzīʿ, 1996 CE / 1417 AH), Ahlulbayt Library 2.0, 378-379.

[176] *Al-Sajjād*

[177] That is the 4th Imam

[178] Aḥmad ibn Muḥammad ibn Ibrāhīm Ibn Khallikān (d. 681 AH), *Wafiyyāt al-Aʿyān wa Anbāʾ Abnāʾ al-Zamān*, ed. Iḥsān ʿAbbās, 2nd ed., vol. 3 (Qom: Manshūrāt al-Sharīf al-Raḍī), Noor Digital Library, 269.

[179] *Khulafāʾ* (sing. *khalīfah*)

[180] 3rd Imam: Ḥusayn son of ʿAlī (4 AH - 61 AH)
Muḥammad ibn Muḥammad ibn al-Nuʿmān al-Mufīd (d. 413 AH), *al-Irshād*, 2nd ed., vol. 2 (Beirut: Dār al-Mufīd lil-Ṭibāʿah wa al-Nashr wa al-Tawzīʿ, 1414 AH / 1993 CE), Ahlulbayt Library 2.0, 27, 133.

[181] I am keeping the original Arabic of this word instead of a translation in order to emphasize that what Prophet Muḥammad is saying here depends on what layers of meaning/application are intended by *sibṭ*;
According to *Lisān al-ʿArab*, there are a number of possible meanings, including: son of a son; son of a daughter; tribe; group; community;
Muḥammad ibn Mukarram Ibn Manẓūr (d. 711 AH), *Lisān al-ʿArab*, vol. 7 (Qom: Nashr Adab al-Ḥawzah, 1405 AH), Ahlulbayt Library 2.0, 310.

[182] *The aṣbāt* (sing. *sibṭ*); the article *"al"* preceding the plural form of *sibṭ* may be referring the listener to a previously recognizable usage of the word *al-asbāṭ*, such as in the Qur'ān.

[183] Muḥammad ibn 'Īsá al-Tirmidhī (d. 279 AH), *Sunan al-Tirmidhī*, ed. 'Abd Al-Raḥmān Muḥammad 'Uthmān, 2nd ed., vol. 5 (Beirut: Dār al-Fikr lil-Ṭibā'ah wa al-Nashr wa al-Tawzī', 1403 AH / 1983 CE), Ahlulbayt Library 2.0, 324.

[184] Qur'ān 3:31

[185] sing. *sibṭ*

[186] See, for instance, Qur'ān 2:140 and 7:159-160

[187] That is the plural form of *sibṭ*: *asbāṭ*

[188] For an intriguing interpretation possibility, see:
Sāmī Al-Badrī, *Shubuhāt wa Rudūd*, 2nd ed., vol. 3 (Nashr Ḥabīb, 1417 AH), Ahlulbayt Library 2.0, 99-100.

[189] The 2nd Imam; Imam Ḥusayn's brother

[190] The 3rd Imam

[191] Or masters

[192] Their mother, the daughter of the last *chosen one*, and the wife of the 1st Imam.

[193] Aḥmad Ibn Ḥanbal (d. 241 AH), *Musnad Aḥmad*, vol. 5 (Beirut: Dār Ṣādir), Ahlulbayt Library 2.0, 391.

[194] 2nd Imam: Ḥasan son of 'Alī (3 AH – 50 AH)
Muḥammad ibn Muḥammad ibn al-Nu'mān al-Mufīd (d. 413 AH), *al-Irshād*, 2nd ed., vol. 2 (Beirut: Dār al-Mufīd lil-

Ṭibāʿah wa al-Nashr wa al-Tawzīʿ, 1414 AH / 1993 CE), Ahlulbayt Library 2.0, 5, 15.

195 Muslim ibn al-Ḥajjāj al-Qushayrī al-Naysābūrī (d. 261 AH), *Ṣaḥīḥ Muslim*, vol. 7 (Beirut: Dār al-Fikr), Ahlulbayt Library 2.0, 129.

196 Qurʾān 53:2-4

197 The 2nd Imam

198 The 3rd Imam; Imam Ḥasan's brother

199 Or masters

200 The 1st Imam

201 Muḥammad ibn ʿAbd Allāh al-Ḥākim al-Naysābūrī (d. 405 AH), *al-Mustadrak ʿalá al-Ṣaḥīḥayn*, ed. Yūsuf ʿAbd al-Raḥmān al-Marʿashlī, vol. 3 (Beirut: Dār al-Maʿrifah), Ahlulbayt Library 2.0, 167.

202 1st Imam: ʿAlī ibn Abī Ṭālib (ca 23 BH – 40 AH) Muḥammad ibn Muḥammad ibn al-Nuʿmān al-Mufīd (d. 413 AH), *al-Irshād*, 2nd ed., vol. 1 (Beirut: Dār al-Mufīd lil-Ṭibāʿah wa al-Nashr wa al-Tawzīʿ, 1414 AH / 1993 CE), Ahlulbayt Library 2.0, 5, 9.

203 *Hārūn*

204 *Mūsá*

205 Muslim ibn al-Ḥajjāj al-Qushayrī al-Naysābūrī (d. 261 AH), *Ṣaḥīḥ Muslim*, vol. 7 (Beirut: Dār al-Fikr), Ahlulbayt Library 2.0, 120.

206 Qurʾān 33:40

207 Qurʾān 25:35

208 Qur'ān 7:142

209 A special place at some stage in the life beyond this world

210 Muḥammad ibn 'Abd Allāh al-Ḥākim al-Naysābūrī (d. 405 AH), *al-Mustadrak 'alá al-Ṣaḥīḥayn*, ed. Yūsuf 'Abd al-Raḥmān al-Mar'ashlī, vol. 3 (Beirut: Dār al-Ma'rifah), Ahlulbayt Library 2.0, 124.

BIBLIOGRAPHY

Al-ʿAmīdī, Thāmir. *Difāʿ ʿAn al-Kāfī*. 1st ed. Vol. 1-2. Markaz al-Ghadīr lil-Dirāsāt al-Islāmiyyah, 1415 AH. PDF.

Al-Aṣfahānī (d. 430 AH), Aḥmad ibn ʿAbd Allāh. *Ḥilyat al-Awliyāʾ wa Ṭabaqāt al-Aṣfiyāʾ*. Vol. 3. Beirut: Dār al-Fikr lil-Ṭibāʿah wa al-Nashr wa al-Tawzīʿ, 1996 CE / 1416 AH. PDF.

Al-Badrī, Sāmī. *Manāhij Khamsah Fī al-Istidlāl ʿAlá Imāmat Ahl al-Bayt (ʿa)*. 1st ed. Baghdad: Dār Ṭūr Sīnīn lil-Ṭibāʿah wa al-Nashr, 1421 AH / 2000 CE. http://albadri.info/books/emameh5/index.htm.

Al-Badrī, Sāmī. *Shubuhāt wa Rudūd*. 2nd ed. Vol. 1-3. Nashr Ḥabīb, 1417 AH. Ahlulbayt Library 2.0.

Al-Dhahabī (d. 748 AH), Shams al-Dīn Muḥammad ibn Aḥmad. *Al-ʿIbar Fī Khabar Man Ghabar*. Edited by Muḥammad Al-Saʿīd Zaghlūl. Vol. 1. Beirut:

Dār al-Kutub al-ʿIlmiyyah, 1985 CE / 1405 AH. PDF.

Al-Dhahabī (d. 748 AH), Shams al-Dīn Muḥammad ibn Aḥmad. *Tārīkh al-Islām*. Edited by ʿUmar ʿAbd Al-Salām Tudmurī. 1st ed. Vol. 15. Beirut: Dār al-Kitāb al-ʿArabī, 1987 CE / 1407 AH. Ahlulbayt Library 2.0.

Al-Ghazālī (d. 505 AH), Muḥammad ibn Muḥammad. *Al-Mustaṣfá fī ʿIlm al-Uṣūl*. Edited by Muḥammad ʿAbd al-Salām ʿAbd al-Shāfī. Beirut: Dār al-Kutub al-ʿIlmiyyah, 1996 CE / 1417 AH. Ahlulbayt Library 2.0.

Al-Ḥākim al-Naysābūrī (d. 405 AH), Muḥammad ibn ʿAbd Allāh. *Al-Mustadrak ʿalá al-Ṣaḥīḥayn*. Edited by Yūsuf ʿAbd Al-Raḥmān al-Marʿashlī. Vol. 1-4. Beirut: Dār al-Maʿrifah. Ahlulbayt Library 2.0.

Al-Ḥamawī (d. 626 AH), Shihāb al-Dīn Yāqūt. *Muʿjam al-Buldān*. Vol. 4. Beirut: Dār Iḥyāʾ al-Turāth al-ʿArabī, 1979 CE / 1399 AH. Ahlulbayt Library 2.0.

Al-Ḥusaynī al-Jalālī, Muḥammad Ḥusayn. *Fihris al-Turāth*. Edited by Muḥammad Jawād Al-Ḥusaynī Al-Jalālī. 1st ed. Vol. 1-2. Qom: Dalīl Mā, 1422 AH. Ahlulbayt Library 2.0.

Al-Ḥusaynī al-Jalālī, Muḥammad Riḍā. *Jihād al-Imām al-Sajjād Zayn al-ʿĀbidīn ʿAlī ibn al-Ḥusayn ibn ʿAlī ibn Abī Ṭālib ʿAlayhim al-Salām*. 1st ed. Dār al-Ḥadīth, 1418 AH. PDF.

Al-Jāḥiẓ (d. 255 AH), ʿAmr ibn Baḥr. *Rasāʾil al-Jāḥiẓ*. Compiled by Ḥasan Al-Sindūbī. 1st ed. Al-Maktabah al-Tijāriyyah al-Kubrá, 1933 CE / 1352 AH. Accessed June 5, 2017. Bibliotheca Alexandrina. Keyword: http://dar.bibalex.org/webpages/dar.jsf.

Al-Jazarī (d. 833 AH), Abū al-Khayr Shams al-Dīn Muḥammad. *Asná al-Maṭālib fī Manāqib Sayyidinā ʿAlī ibn Abī Ṭālib*. Edited by Muḥammad Hādī Al-Amīnī. Isfahān: Maktabat al-Imām Amīr al-Muʾminīn ʿalayh al-Salām al-ʿĀmmah. Electronic.

Al-Jurjānī (d. 365 AH), Abū Aḥmad ʿAbd Allāh ibn ʿUday. *Al-Kāmil Fī Ḍuʿafāʾ al-Rijāl*. Edited by Suhayl Zakkār and Yaḥyá Mukhtār Ghazzāwī. 3rd ed. Vol. 1-7. Beirut: Dār al-Fikr lil-Ṭibāʿah wa al-Nashr wa al-Tawzīʿ, 1998 CE / 1409 AH.

Al-Khaṭīb al-Baghdādī (d. 463 AH), Aḥmad ibn ʿAlī. *Tārīkh Baghdād*. Edited by Muṣṭafá ʿAbd Al-Qādir ʿAṭā. 1st ed. Vol. 13. Beirut: Dār al-Kutub al-ʿIlmiyyah, 1997 CE / 1417 AH. Ahlulbayt Library 2.0.

Al-Kulaynī (d. ca. 329 AH / 941 CE), Abū Jaʿfar Muḥammad ibn Yaʿqūb. *Al-Kāfī*. Edited by ʿAlī Akbar al-Ghaffārī. 4th ed. Vol. 1-8. Tehran: Dār al-Kutub al-Islāmīyah, 1984 CE. Ahlulbayt Library 2.0.

Al-Mālikī (d. 855 AH), Ibn al-Ṣabbāgh. *Al-Fuṣūl al-Muhimmah Fī Maʿrifat al-Aʾimmah*. Edited by Sāmī Al-Gharīrī. 1st ed. Vol. 2. Qom: Dār al-Ḥadīth lil-

Ṭibāʿah wa al-Nashr, 1422 AH. Ahlulbayt Library 2.0.

Al-Masʿūdī (d. ca 345 AH), Abū al-Ḥasan ʿAlī ibn al-Ḥusayn. *Ithbāt al-Waṣiyyah*. 2nd ed. Beirut: Dār al-Aḍwāʾ lil-Ṭibāʿah wa al-Nashr wa al-Tawzīʿ, 1988 CE / 1409 AH. PDF.

Al-Mufīd (d. 413 AH), Muḥammad ibn Muḥammad ibn al-Nuʿmān. *Al-Irshād*. 2nd ed. Vol. 1-2. Beirut: Dār al-Mufīd lil-Ṭibāʿah wa al-Nashr wa al-Tawzīʿ, 1414 AH / 1993 CE. Ahlulbayt Library 2.0.

Al-Nūrī al-Ṭabarsī (d. 1320 AH), Ḥusayn. *Kashf al-Astār ʿAn Wajh al-Ghāʾib ʿAn al-Abṣār*. 2nd ed. Qom: Maṭbaʿat al-Khiyām, 1400 AH. PDF.

Al-Qummī al-Ṣadūq (d. 381 AH), Abū Jaʿfar Muḥammad ibn ʿAlī ibn al-Ḥusayn ibn Bābawayh. *Kamāl al-Dīn wa Tamām al-Niʿmah*. Edited by ʿAlī Akbar Al-Ghaffārī. Qom: Muʾassasat al-Nashr al-Islāmī, 1405 AH. Ahlulbayt Library 2.0.

Al-Qushayrī al-Naysābūrī (d. 261 AH), Muslim ibn al-Ḥajjāj. *Ṣaḥīḥ Muslim*. Vol. 1-8. Beirut: Dār al-Fikr. Ahlulbayt Library 2.0.

Al-Raḥmah, Ḥikmat. *Aʾimmah Ahl al-Bayt ʿalayhim al-Salām fī Kutub Ahl al-Sunnah*. Qom: Muʾassasat al-Kawthar lil-Maʿārif al-Islāmiyyah. Electronic.

Al-Ṣafadī (d. 764 AH), Ṣalāḥ al-Dīn Khalīl ibn Aybak. *Al-Wāfī bil-Wafiyāt*. Edited by Aḥmad Al-Arnāʾūt and Turkī Muṣtafá. Vol. 1-29. Beirut: Dār Iḥyāʾ al-

Turāth, 2000 CE / 1420 AH. Ahlulbayt Library 2.0.

Al-Ṣāfī al-Gulpaygānī, Luṭf Allāh. *Muntakhab al-Athar Fī al-Imām al-Thānī ʿAshar ʿAlayh al-Salām*. 1st ed. Vol. 1-3. Qom: Maktabat Āyat Allāh al-ʿUẓmá al-Ṣāfī al-Gulpaygānī, Waḥdat al-Nashr al-ʿĀlamiyyah, 1422 AH. May 19, 2013. Accessed June 3, 2017. http://www.m-mahdi.net/main/books-120; http://www.m-mahdi.net/main/books-121; http://www.m-mahdi.net/main/books-122

Al-Shāfiʿī (d. 652 AH), Muḥammad ibn Ṭalḥah. *Maṭālib al-Saʾūl Fī Manāqib Āl al-Rasūl*. Edited by Mājid Aḥmad Al-ʿAṭiyyah. Vol. 1. Ahlulbayt Library 2.0.

Al-Tirmidhī (d. 279 AH), Muḥammad ibn ʿĪsá. *Sunan al-Tirmidhī*. Edited by ʿAbd Al-Raḥmān Muḥammad ʿUthmān. 2nd ed. Vol. 1-5. Beirut: Dār al-Fikr lil-Ṭibāʿah wa al-Nashr wa al-Tawzīʿ, 1403 AH / 1983 CE. Ahlulbayt Library 2.0.

Al-Yaḥṣibī (d. 544 AH), ʿIyāḍ ibn Mūsá. *Al-Shifā bi Taʿrīf Ḥuqūq al-Muṣṭafá*. Vol. 1-2. Beirut: Dār al-Fikr lil-Ṭibāʿah wa al-Nashr wa al-Tawzīʿ, 1988 CE / 1409 AH. Ahlulbayt Library 2.0.

Fakhr al-Dīn al-Rāzī (d. 606 AH), Muḥammad ibn ʿUmar. *Tafsīr al-Rāzī*. 3rd ed. Vol. 32. Ahlulbayt Library 2.0.

Ibn Abī al-Ḥadīd (d. 656 AH), ʿAbd al-Ḥamīd. *Sharḥ Nahj al-Balāghah*. Edited by Muḥammad Abū Al-Faḍl

Ibrāhīm. 1st ed. Vol. 15. Dār Iḥyā' al-Kutub al-'Arabiyyah, 1962 CE. Ahlulbayt Library 2.0.

Ibn Abī al-Ḥadīd (d. 656 AH), 'Abd al-Ḥamīd. *Sharḥ Nahj al-Balāghah*. Edited by Muḥammad Abū Al-Faḍl Ibrāhīm. 1st ed. Vol. 2. Dār Iḥyā' al-Kutub al-'Arabiyyah, 1378 AH / 1959 CE. Ahlulbayt Library 2.0.

Ibn Abī Ḥātim al-Rāzī (d. 327 AH), 'Abd al-Raḥmān. *Al-Jarḥ wa al-Ta'dīl*. 1st ed. Vol. 8. Beirut: Dār Iḥyā' al-Turāth al-'Arabī, 1953 CE / 1372 AH. Ahlulbayt Library 2.0.

Ibn 'Asākir, 'Alī ibn al-Ḥasan ibn Hibat Allāh. *Tārīkh Madīnat Dimashq*. Edited by 'Alī Shīrī. 1st ed. Vol. 1-70. Beirut: Dār al-Fikr lil-Ṭibā'ah wa al-Nashr wa al-Tawzī', 1996 CE / 1417 AH. Ahlulbayt Library 2.0.

Ibn Ḥanbal (d. 241 AH), Aḥmad. *Musnad Aḥmad*. Vol. 1-6. Beirut: Dār Ṣādir. Ahlulbayt Library 2.0.

Ibn Ḥibbān (d. 354 AH), Muḥammad. *Al-Thuqāt*. 1st ed. Vol. 8. Hyderabad Deccan: Dā'irat al-Ma'ārif al-'Uthmāniyyah, 1982 CE / 1402 AH. Ahlulbayt Library 2.0.

Ibn Khallikān (d. 681 AH), Aḥmad ibn Muḥammad ibn Ibrāhīm. *Wafiyyāt al-A'yān wa Anbā' Abnā' al-Zamān*. Edited by Iḥsān 'Abbās. 2nd ed. Vol. 1-8. Qom: Manshūrāt al-Sharīf al-Raḍī. Noor Digital Library.

Ibn Manẓūr (d. 711 AH), Muḥammad ibn Mukarram. *Lisān al-ʿArab.* Vol. 1-15. Qom: Nashr Adab al-Ḥawzah, 1405 AH. Ahlulbayt Library 2.0.

Sibṭ ibn al-Jawzī (d. 654 AH), Yūsuf ibn ʿAbd Allāh. *Tadhkirat al-Khawāṣ.* Tehran: Maktabat Nīnawá al-Ḥadīthah. PDF.

www.ingramcontent.com/pod-product-compliance
Lightning Source LLC
Chambersburg PA
CBHW032141040426
42449CB00005B/351
* 9 7 8 1 9 4 3 3 9 3 3 9 8 *